Kids
to the Rescue!
First Aid Techniques for Kids

Revised Edition

Maribeth & Darwin Boelts

Illustrated by Marina Megale

PARENTING PRESS, INC.

Acknowledgments

The authors would like to thank the Boy Scouts of America, Irving, Texas; the American Heart Association, Dallas, Texas; and Sara Van Brocklin, a ten-year-old reader and friend.

The publisher would like to thank Dr. Jeffrey Lindenbaum of Group Health, Seattle, Washington; Ron Rutherford, Ph.D. of Lifetek, Inc., Kirkland, Washington; and Dr. Paul Mendelman, University of Washington School of Medicine, Department of Pediatrics, Seattle, Washington for their review of the text and first aid procedures. Special thanks also go to Stacey Shiovitz for a youthful review of the text and illustrations.

The illustrator thanks all those who helped model for the drawings: Rosanne and Suzanne Ritch; Matthew, Grant, and Virginia Kolkoske; Jesse and Nicky Wilke; and Sue and Shaunte Marie Gagner. Thanks also to Selene the Snake for photo reference.

Designed by Magrit Baurecht
Printed in the United States of America

Library of Congress Cataloging-in-Publication Data

Boelts, Maribeth, 1964-

Kids to the rescue! : first aid techniques for kids / Maribeth & Darwin Boelts ; illustrated by Marina Megale. Rev. Ed.

p. cm.

Includes index.

Summary: Provides basic instruction in first aid for a variety of accidents and injuries, including nose bleeds, snake bites, and choking, plus information on when and how to call for help.

ISBN 1-884734-79-0   ISBN 1-884734-78-2 (pbk.)

1. First aid in illness and injury   Juvenile literature [1. First aid.] I. Boelts, Darwin. II. Megale, Marina, ill. III. Title.

RC86.5 .B64 2003

616.02'52 dc21   2002030781

PARENTING PRESS, INC.
814 North Franklin Street
Chicago, Illinois 60610
www.parentingpress.com

Contents

Note to Parents and Teachers

Children are natural learners. They like to explore, ask questions, and pretend. They learn by doing.

Kids to the Rescue! First Aid Techniques for Kids is designed to encourage children to:

– **Listen** to the first aid situation as it is read by an adult.
– **Look** at the illustration and visualize themselves in the situation.
– **Role-play** the steps on the first aid page enough times to ensure easy recall.

This book is designed to utilize the adult as a child's helper. You can read the situation to a pre-reading child, or listen as the older child reads the text himself. Then, you can help the child act out the first aid steps. It is important to say, "Yes!" when the child asks if he can run cold water on a "burn" or elevate a "swollen ankle." Pretending and role-playing will help them remember.

You will see children grow in confidence as the first aid steps are mastered. To a child, it is empowering, not scary, to know that bleeding can be stopped by direct pressure and that insect stings can be soothed with cool water. To a parent, it is reassuring to know that your child is capable of dialing an emergency number on the telephone and relaying basic information to the operator.

Teach your children how to dial 911 or your local emergency number for help when there are no able grown-ups nearby. Show them how to look up emergency numbers in the front of the telephone directory.

Record emergency numbers for them on page 71 of this book and post this page (or a copy) by your telephone.

Accidents are the leading cause of death for children ages 1 to 14. Other children are often present when an injury occurs. Knowing what to do right at the moment of injury can dramatically improve a child's chance for recovery.

Now, let's turn to the first situation and get ready to help a child join the other Kids to the Rescue!

Just for Kids

All kids play together. Sometimes when kids play together, one of them gets hurt. A grown-up may not be there to help. Do you know what to do if your friend gets hurt? Do you know how to help if you get hurt?

This book will show you how to help yourself and others. You can learn how to give first aid and get help.

Nose Bleed

You get a new aluminum bat and a real baseball for your birthday.

"Will you pitch some balls to me?" you ask your big brother.

"Sure, as long as you pitch some to me, too," he says.

You walk to the playground by your apartment building. Your brother throws you the first pitch. You hit a pop fly right to him.

"Good hit," he says. "Try to keep it out of the air, though."

He pitches again. This time you hit a ground ball that rolls to the fence.

"That's better. You'd make it to second base on that one," he says. "Last pitch and then it's my turn to bat."

He winds up to pitch and then releases the ball. Your brother's aim is a little off, and the ball hits you right on the nose. You touch your nose. It's bleeding!

How to help with a nose bleed:

❀ **Squeeze your nose and look down.** Take hold of the whole soft part of your nose and pinch it together. As you pinch your nose, look down. Don't tip your head back.

❀ **Squeeze for ten minutes.** Keep squeezing your nose for ten minutes before you let go.

❀ **Check to see if your nose is still bleeding.** If it is, squeeze your nose some more. Check again. If the bleeding hasn't stopped, go get help.

❀ **Even if the bleeding has stopped,** remember to tell a grown-up that you have had a nosebleed.

Squeeze the whole soft part of your nose and look down.

Something in the Eye

Your front yard is covered with a thick blanket of orange, red, and yellow leaves.

"Today would be a good day to rake," your dad says. "Why don't you take the front yard, and I'll work on the back. When we get done, we can go rent that video game you've been wanting to play."

You begin raking, thinking about how you're going to try to beat your dad at the video game later that evening. You don't notice the large gray clouds that are beginning to appear in the sky. The air feels funny, like it might rain. A strong gust of wind suddenly blows your pile of leaves up into the air. The wind stirs up dirt and dust in the yard. You blink, but a tiny piece of a leaf and some of the dust gets in your eye.

How to help with something in the eye:

❊ **Leave your eye alone.** Do not rub or touch your eyeball. The dirt could scratch your eye and make it hurt worse.

❊ **Use your eyelid to help.** Gently take hold of your upper eyelid and pull it carefully over the bottom eyelid. Then, still holding your eyelid, blink.

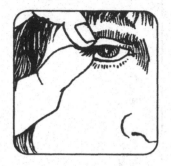

❊ **Rinse your eye.** If using your eyelid didn't help, use water to rinse your eye. Hold your eye under a faucet or hose and rinse it with cold water. Be careful that the water doesn't run into your other eye.

❊ **Go for help.** If your eye still doesn't feel better, go ask someone for help.

HINT

Do not rub your eye.

Bleeding

Your cousin from Florida is visiting you for the week.

"It's warmer in Florida than it is in Maine," she says, shivering. "And your beaches are rockier."

"We can go back to my house to get your jacket and shoes," you offer.

"No, I'm okay," she answers. "The last time you visited me in Florida, I showed you my shell collection. Let's see if we can find some that I can add to it when I get home." She runs up ahead to check out what looks like a beautiful, shiny shell. Suddenly, she stops and grabs her foot. "Ow! What did I step on?" she exclaims.

You catch up with her and see blood flowing from her heel. It's making a red puddle in the sand. In that puddle is a piece of glass from a broken bottle.

How to help with bleeding:

❊ **Do not touch the cut yourself.**
Blood can carry serious diseases.
Show your cousin how to press
on the cut. Tell her to press
until the bleeding stops. If she
has a clean scarf or tissue, she
can put that on the cut before
she starts to press on it. Never
wrap or tie anything around
the cut to stop the bleeding.

❊ **Elevate the cut.** Tell your cousin
to sit down. You can raise her
foot by putting something
under it. You could roll your
jacket up or use a backpack to
put underneath her cut foot.

❊ **Go for help.** Tell your cousin to
keep pushing on the cut. Call
or go find help for her.

HINT

**Press right on the cut
and elevate it.**

Broken Bones

You are riding on the bike trail near your home. "Come on, I'll race you to the bridge!" you shout to your friend. Your friend accepts the challenge and speeds ahead. The trees and flowers along the trail become a blur as you pump the pedals, but your friend is still winning!

As he turns around to see how far back you are, his bike heads straight for a large rock alongside the trail. He hits the rock and is thrown off his bike. You race over to help him. You notice that his arm is bent in a funny way. Your friend is crying because his arm hurts so much.

How to help with broken bones:

❀ **Yell for help!** A broken bone needs attention from a doctor.

❀ **Keep the hurt arm still.** Don't move it. The bone may be broken. Tell your friend to stay exactly where he fell, unless it's a dangerous place.

❀ **Check for bleeding.** If your friend has a cut, remember how to help. Have him press on the cut until the bleeding stops. Do not press on his cut yourself.

HINT

Call for help and don't move a bone that might be broken.

Dog Bite

You wake up one morning and glance sleepily at the clock. "Only 15 minutes to get ready for school!" you exclaim as you hop out of bed.

After a quick bowl of cereal and a few minutes spent brushing your teeth, combing your hair, and getting dressed, you head out the door.

You decide to take a shortcut to school. Halfway through an empty lot, you hear the low, throaty growl of a dog. You turn to face him, and you notice that his teeth are bared and his tail isn't wagging. You haven't seen him on your way to school before. You forget that you aren't supposed to move suddenly in front of an angry dog and you start to run. The dog chases you and then bites you on the arm.

How to help with a dog bite:

✾ **Notice what kind of dog bit you.** Look at it carefully. How big is it? What color fur does it have? Does it have long or short fur? Have you seen the dog before? If so, where?

✾ **Check for bleeding.** If the bite mark is bleeding, press on it to stop the bleeding. Wash the bite. Hold it under cold water.

✾ **Call or go for help.** A grown-up will need to know that you have been bitten by a dog. You will need to describe the dog so grown-ups can find it.

HINT

**Notice what the dog looks like,
and find a grown-up right away.**

Snake Bite

It's the last day of summer camp. You and your best friend want to do something fun during the free period in the afternoon.

"Do you want to climb on the rocks in back of the lodge?" she asks.

"Sure, that sounds great," you reply.

After you tell the camp counselor where you will be, you both climb to the top of the rocks. You talk about the letters you'll write each other when you get back home. The time passes quickly.

"I think the free period is over," your friend says. "We should start heading back." She climbs down the rocks. Suddenly, she cries out. "A snake just bit me!" she screams.

You stop just in time to see a snake slither by.

How to help with a snake bite:

❋ **Lie down.** Your friend should lie down and try to stay very still. Keep the part of her body that was bitten lower than her chest. This will keep the poison from reaching her heart too fast.

❋ **Remember what the snake looks like and stay quiet.** A snake bite is a scary thing for both of you. You will help your friend by telling her that she will be okay. Say, "I'll find help. Don't move until I get back. It will be okay."

Get help. Yell for help, or go find help quickly. Tell a grown-up what the snake looked like, what color it was, and how big it was.

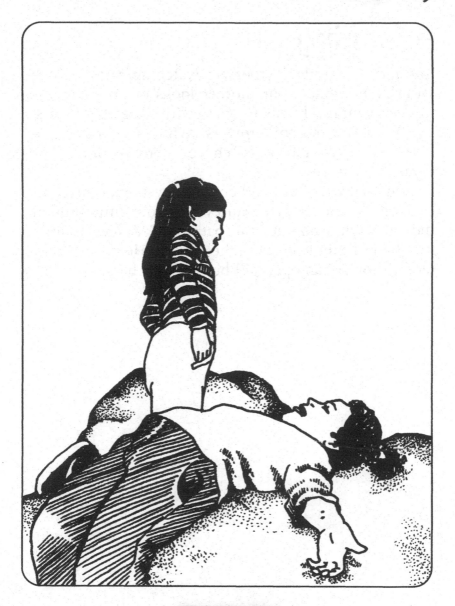

HINT

Lie down and keep the part of the body that was bitten lower than the chest.

Poisoning

You and your little brother are watching cartoons one Saturday morning. Your mother looks out the window and sees your neighbor struggling with a bag of groceries.

"I'm going out to help Mrs. Winters with her groceries. Will you please watch your brother for a few minutes?" she asks.

You nod your head and continue watching cartoons. You forget about keeping an eye on your little brother and he toddles off into the bathroom. A few minutes later he walks in front of the television. He says, "Yucky candy." You see an open pill bottle in his hand.

How to help with poisoning:

❋ **Take the pill bottle away.** Keep it away from your brother, but close by. You will need to know what kind of pills he ate when you call the poison control center.

❋ **Call for help.** If you cannot find your parents or another grown-up, dial 911 or your emergency number. Then call the poison control center to find out what to do next.

❋ **Watch carefully.** Taking too many pills may make a child vomit. Other pills may make him sleepy. Keep your brother close by, and when help arrives, you can tell the grown-up how your brother has been acting.

HINT

When someone eats or drinks something that could be poisonous, call the emergency number and the poison control center number.

Insect Sting

You and your father are busy loading the car for a camping trip. You don't notice when your new kitten Smoky darts out the front door. After everything is in the car, you can't find Smoky. You start looking around the house, but you can't find her. You decide to try looking outside.

"Smoky!" you call. "Smoky!"

As you cut across the driveway to your neighbor's flower garden, you hear a soft mewing. Bending low, you part the bushy flowers with your hands.

"Smoky?" you say. Two little green eyes peer out at you. As you reach for your kitten, a bee lands on your arm. Before you know it, the bee stings you.

"Ouch!" you cry, grabbing your arm with your other hand. Smoky is startled and quickly hides under the bush again.

How to help with an insect sting:

✽ **Shout for help.** If you are allergic to bee stings, get help quickly.

✽ **Put the part of the body that was stung under cold water.** Run the water on the insect sting until it feels a little better. If you are allergic to bee stings, call 911 or your local emergency number. Or ask someone else to call for you. If you are not allergic, you can help yourself safely.

HINT

Put the part of the body that was stung under cold water.

Chemical Burns in the Eye

It's moving day and everyone is busy. Your mom and dad run next door to the neighbors' to see if they have any extra boxes. You and your friend are supposed to pack up the few things left in the kitchen.

"Don't forget that stuff still on top of the refrigerator," your friend reminds you.

"That's just what I was going to do," you say. Standing on your tiptoes, you reach for the top of the refrigerator. As you feel around for the items, you knock over a bottle of kitchen cleanser. The loose lid comes off and cleanser gets into your friend's eye.

How to help with chemicals in the eye:

❀ **Run cool water on the eye.** Quickly, lead your friend to a sink. Tell him to lean over and put his hurt eye under the cold water from the faucet. Be careful that the water doesn't run into his other eye.

❀ **Get help.** Call your parents or another grown-up while your friend rinses his eye.

❀ **Run cold water on his eye for 15 minutes.** You can set a timer to help you.

HINT

Run cool water on the
eye right away.

Choking

"Hey, your dad packed us a pretty good lunch," your friend says, as he unwraps three tuna fish sandwiches, a bunch of grapes, and a bag of cookies from the basket.

"We deserve it after the hiking we've done," your other friend tells him.

"How much farther till we reach Pyramid Peak?" you ask.

"I think we're about halfway there. The sooner we finish lunch, the sooner we'll get there. Maybe we'll beat that group that's behind us," your friend says.

You quickly begin eating your lunch. One of your friends wolfs down his sandwich and pops a few grapes into his mouth. Suddenly, he grasps his throat. He can't talk or breathe. "Is he choking?" your other friend asks worriedly.

How to help with choking:

❋ **Get behind your friend and position your hands.**

    1. Place one hand on his shoulder and use the finger of your other hand to find his belly button.

    2. Place your fist above his belly button, then grab your fist with your other hand.

❋ **Let your friend hang over your fists and thrust in, very hard, six to ten times.** If he still can't breathe, try again.

❋ **Send for help.** Your other friend can find a grown-up or call 911 or the local emergency number.

HINT

**Place fist above belly button; grab fist
with your other hand; thrust in very
hard, six to ten times.**

Electric Shock

Your mother has invited a friend and her two-year-old daughter over for lunch. After lunch, your mother asks you to play with the little girl up in your bedroom.

"Do you want to make a picture for your mom?" you ask. She smiles and nods her head.

"Okay. I'll cut and you can glue," you say.

There is an extra pair of scissors in your coloring box. While you are busy, the little girl takes the scissors and sticks them into the outlet on the wall. She screams and can't seem to let go of the scissors.

How to help with electric shock:

❀ **DON'T TOUCH HER!** Stay away from her. You, too, could get shocked if you touch her, and then you couldn't help her.

❀ **Get help right away.** Ask a grown-up to push her away from the outlet with a wooden chair or broom. A grown-up can also shut off the electricity in the house.

HINT

**Never touch someone who is being shocked.
Get help right away.**

Burns

Your family shares a garden space with your neighbors.

"How about corn on the cob for supper tonight?" your mom asks.

"Great!" you answer. "Do you want me to go next door and pick some?"

"No, but I would like you to stay here in the house and let me know when this pot of water boils. I should have the corn picked by then," she says.

The pot of water simmers on the stove. Soon, there are little bubbles forming around the edges of the pot. You notice that the handle of the pot is facing the front of the stove. You decide to turn the handle toward the back of the stove. The pot tips as you turn it and some boiling hot water splashes onto your arm.

How to help with burns:

✳ **Put your hurt arm in cold water right away.** Hold it under the faucet or put it in a pan of cold water. Keep your burn in cold water until it stops hurting. It may take as long as 30 minutes to cool your burn.

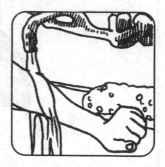

✳ **Call a grown-up.** If the burn still hurts when it's out of the cold water, call your mother or father, or another grown-up, to help.

HINT

Put a burn in cold water.

Unconsciousness

You are helping your aunt paint the living room in her new apartment.

"If you paint the low parts, I'll paint the high parts," she says. Then she climbs an old wooden ladder and begins to paint the ceiling. In just a short while the ceiling is covered with fresh, white paint.

"There," she says. "Do you see any place that I missed?" You see a dull, gray patch in the corner and point it out to her.

"No problem. I'll just move the ladder over and get that one spot," she says. As she quickly climbs back up the ladder and reaches up to paint, the ladder slips out from under her. She falls with a heavy thud to the ground.

You rush over to her. "Aunt Cathy!" you shout, but she does not answer or move. It is like she is asleep, but will not wake up. You wonder, is she unconscious?

How to help with unconsciousness:

❊ **Don't touch her.** Do not try to move her.

❊ **Call for help.** If a grown-up is close by, ask for help.

❊ **Dial the emergency number.** Say, "My aunt fell and won't wake up." The dispatcher will ask you for your address and phone number, and tell you what to do next.

HINT

**Don't move an unconscious person.
Call for help right away.**

Clothing on Fire

It is the last campout of the summer. The fire is blazing and the night sky is full of stars. You are roasting marshmallows with your family and talking about all the fun things you did over the summer.

As you talk, you notice that your sister's marshmallow is on fire.

"Here, I'll blow it out for you," you say as you take it away from her. While you are helping her, your pant leg gets too close to the flames and catches on fire!

How to help with clothing on fire:

❋ **STOP.** Freeze — don't move! Running will make the fire burn faster.

❋ **DROP.** Lie down on the ground right away.

❋ **ROLL.** Roll back and forth on the ground to put the fire out.

❋ **Yell for help.** If people are close by, tell them to pour water on your clothes.

If your skin gets burned, remember how to take care of a burn. See page 52. You may also need medical care from a doctor.

HINT

If your clothing catches on fire,
STOP, DROP, and ROLL.

Using the Telephone to Get Help

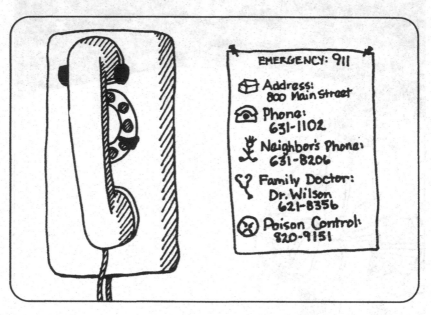

EMERGENCY: 911

Address: 800 Main Street

Phone: 631-1102

Neighbor's Phone: 631-8206

Family Doctor: Dr. Wilson 621-8356

Poison Control: 820-9151

You can practice calling 911, the emergency number for most towns in the United States, by pretending to call on a toy phone, or on a real, disconnected phone. If your town uses a different emergency number, look it up in the front of your phone book. A grown-up can help you practice. Remember, we call the emergency number *only when we truly need help.*

If you are in a situation where someone is hurt and you can't find a grown-up to help, dial 911 or your local emergency number. Do not call the number unless you really need help.

After a grown-up fills out the information on the emergency form on page 71, hang it near your phone. It would be a good idea to practice dialing the emergency number and the numbers of your neighbor, family doctor, and the poison control center.

Using the telephone, step by step:

❋ **Dial the emergency number**

_____.

❋ **Tell the person who answers your name, address, and phone number.** You can say "My **name** is

_____.

My **address** is

_____.

My **phone number** is

"
_____.

❋ **Tell the person why you need help.** Stay on the phone until the person who answered it tells you to hang up.

HINT

Give the person who answers your name, address, and phone number. Then say what is the matter.

Congratulations! You have just completed *Kids to the Rescue!* But wait a minute . . . do you think that you will remember all that you've learned? Do you know what will help you remember everything?

Practice!

Keep this book in a place where you can find it easily. Use your little brother or sister, your best friend, or even your stuffed animal as a pretend patient. Talk through the first aid steps as you act them out. If you can't remember the steps, look at your book, or ask a grown-up for help.

Use the quiz on the next pages to test yourself. Then keep practicing. You never know when you'll need to be a "kid to the rescue!"

First Aid Quiz

Choose the best answer to these first aid questions. If you are stumped, look for the answer in the book or in the answer key.

1. A good way to stop bleeding from a cut is to . . .
   A. Press next to the cut.
   B. Press on the cut.
   C. Run cold water on the cut.

2. If you burn yourself on a hot cookie sheet, you should . . .
   A. Press on the burn.
   B. Rub butter on the burn.
   C. Hold the burn under cold water until it feels better.

3. Your friend falls off a jungle gym. His leg looks funny. You should . . .
   A. Try to straighten the leg.
   B. Move him out from under the jungle gym.
   C. Shout for help. If no one comes, then go for help.

4. Someone is knocked unconscious. You should . . .
   A. Try to "wake her up."
   B. Move her to where she might be more comfortable.
   C. Call for help.

5. If you get something in your eye and you rub it, it could scratch the surface of your eye.
   A. True
   B. False

6. If your friend gets a chemical splashed in his eye, you should help him by having him rinse his eye for . . .
   A. 1 minute
   B. 15 minutes
   C. 5 minutes

7. **When you are helping someone who is choking, where do you put your fists?**
   A. Just above his belly button.
   B. Just below his belly button.
   C. In your pockets.

8. **Your nose starts to bleed while you are practicing cartwheels. You should . . .**
   A. Tilt your head back.
   B. Put a tissue in your nose to plug it.
   C. Pinch the whole soft part of your nose together and lean forward.

9. **If you touch someone who is getting an electrical shock, you will get shocked too.**
   A. True
   B. False

10. **Cold water on an insect sting will help the pain.**
    A. True
    B. False

11. **Your baby brother eats some poison by accident. The first thing you should do is . . .**
    A. Take away the poison.
    B. Call for help.

12. **If you are bitten by a dog, try to remember . . .**
    A. The size of the dog.
    B. The color of the dog.
    C. If you have seen the dog before.
    D. All of the above.

13. **Your clothes are on fire! You should . . .**
    A. Run and try to find water to put it out.
    B. Stop, drop, and roll.
    C. Try to take off the burning clothes.

14. **Your friend is bleeding. You should . . .**
    A. Press your hand on the cut.
    B. Tie something tightly around the cut.
    C. Tell your friend to press his hand on the cut.

Answer Key

Now check your answers below.

1. B. If you are bleeding, the quickest way to stop it is to press on the cut.

2. C. Cold water helps a burn.

3. C. Never try to move or straighten a hurt arm or leg. Shout or go for help.

4. C. You will need help right away if someone is unconscious.

5. A. True. Rubbing your eye when something is in it can scratch the surface of your eye.

6. B. You should have your friend rinse his eye for 15 minutes.

7. A. You place your fists just above the belly button.

8. C. If your nose starts to bleed, pinch the whole soft part together and lean forward.

9. A. True. Never touch a person who is getting an electrical shock. Call for help right away.

10. A. True. Cold water helps an insect sting feel better.

11. A. Take the poison away first and then call for help.

12. D. If you are bitten by a dog, try to remember as much about the dog as you can.

13. B. The best way to stop a fire is to stop, drop, and roll.

14. C. Never touch someone else's blood. Blood can carry serious diseases you could catch.

Alphabetical Index

EMERGENCY:

 Address:

 Phone:

 Neighbor's Phone:

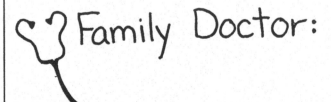 Family Doctor:

 Poison Control: